HOW TALL HOW SHORT HOW FARAWAY

David A. Adler
illustrated by Nancy Tobin

Holiday House / New York

To Hy Ozer,
mathematician, educator, and friend.
D.A.

To my mother.
N.T.

Text copyright © 1999 by David A. Adler
Illustrations copyright © 1999 by Nancy Tobin

Design by Nancy Tobin / Square Moon Productions
All rights reserved
Printed and bound in April 2021 at Toppan Leefung, DongGuan City, China.

15 17 19 20 18 16

Library of Congress Cataloging-in-Publication Data

Adler, David A.
  How tall, how short, how faraway / by David A. Adler;
illustrated by Nancy Tobin. — 1st ed.
  p. cm.
Summary: Introduces several measuring systems such as
the Egyptian system, the inch-pound system, and the
metric system.
  ISBN 0-8234-1375-6
  1. Mensuration — Juvenile literature. [1. Measurement.]
I. Tobin, Nancy, ill. II. Title.
QA465.A26 1999   98-18802
530.8—dc21   CIP
                                                        AC
  ISBN 0-8234-1632-1 (pbk.)

  ISBN-13: 978-0-8234-1375-1 (hardcover)
  ISBN-13: 978-0-8234-1632-5 (pbk)

How tall are you?
How long is your block? How faraway is your school?

The only way to answer these questions is by measuring.
People have been measuring things for thousands of years.

In ancient Egypt, fingers,
hands, and arms were used as
measuring tools.

The width of one finger
was a <u>digit</u>,

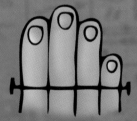

and the width of four fingers
was a <u>palm</u>.

Open your hand. Stretch out your fingers. The distance from the tip of your thumb to the end of your little finger was a <u>span</u>. Now bend your arm. The distance from your elbow to the tip of your middle finger was a <u>cubit</u>.

Try figuring out your height
using the units of measure of ancient Egypt.

Stand straight, with your back against a wall.
Have an adult mark your height with a very light pencil mark.

How many cubits tall are you?

Lie down on the floor. Place your elbow
on the floor next to the wall. Bend it and reach up.
Make a light pencil mark where the tip
of your middle finger
touches the wall.

That's 1 cubit.

Now get up and put your elbow
at the 1-cubit mark. Reach up. Make a light pencil mark
where the tip of your middle finger touches the wall.

That's 2 cubits. Keep measuring cubits.

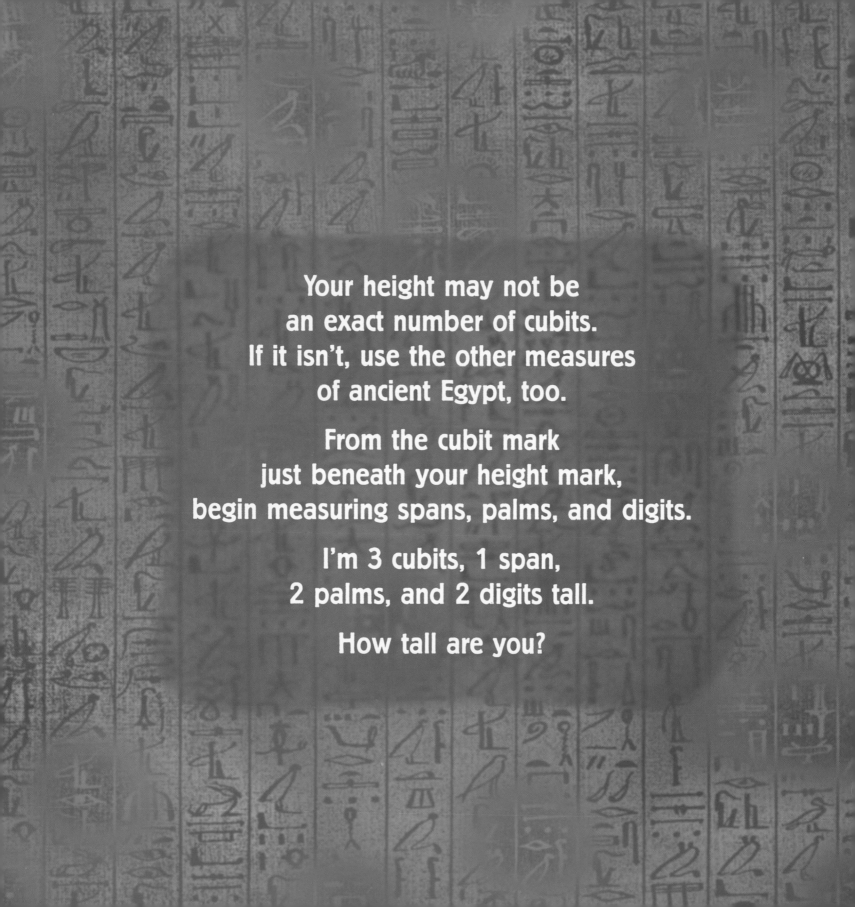

Your height may not be
an exact number of cubits.
If it isn't, use the other measures
of ancient Egypt, too.

From the cubit mark
just beneath your height mark,
begin measuring spans, palms, and digits.

I'm 3 cubits, 1 span,
2 palms, and 2 digits tall.

How tall are you?

Try measuring the
length of your block.

Take your friend and an adult
to one end of your block.
Count your steps as you walk
to the other end.
Every two steps is a <u>pace</u>,
a measure used in ancient Rome.

You, your friend, and the adult walking
with you may each get a different answer.
That's because the length of your steps is different.

If you were to measure a greater distance,
perhaps the distance from your house to your school,
you might measure it in miles. In ancient Rome, one mile
was measured by counting <u>one thousand paces</u>.

If everyone used her own arm to measure,
we wouldn't know the exact size of anything!
If everyone used her own steps to measure paces and miles,
we wouldn't know the exact distance to anyplace.

In the past, people often used one man's cubit or steps as a standard. That man was usually the people's leader or king.

Of course, kings would not travel
from house to house to measure things.
So standard measuring sticks were made.

In different times and parts of the world, there have been many systems of measurement. Today only two systems are widely used.

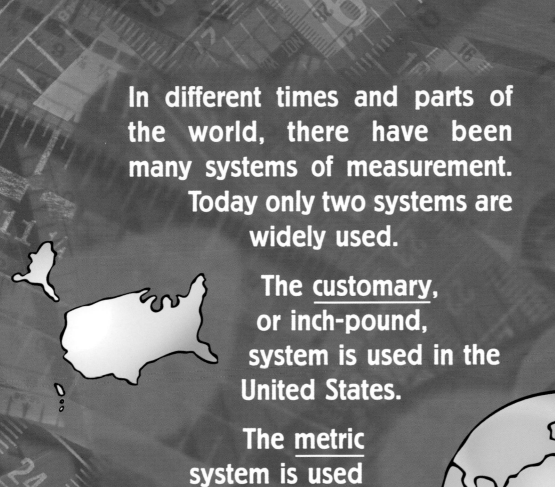

The <u>customary</u>, or inch-pound, system is used in the United States.

The <u>metric</u> system is used almost everywhere else.

The customary system is based on Roman measures.

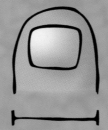

1 inch is about the width of a thumb.

12 inches are 1 foot.

3 feet are 1 yard.

5,280 feet (1,760 yards) are 1 mile.

The metric system
was first proposed over
three hundred years ago
by Father Gabriel Mouton,
a French priest.
The original meter
was not the length of
someone's arm or step.
It was figured as
one ten-millionth of the
distance from the North
Pole to the equator.

All metric measures of length and distance are based
on the meter and the number 10.
A meter is a little more than 39 inches (39.37 inches).

The meter is the basic unit of measure.

10 meters are 1 <u>dekameter</u>.

100 meters are 1 <u>hectometer</u>.

1000 meters are 1 <u>kilometer</u>.

There are units smaller than a meter, too.

1/10 of a meter is a <u>decimeter</u>.

1/100 of a meter is a <u>centimeter</u>.

1/1000 of a meter is a <u>millimeter</u>.

Now open your refrigerator.

Which units of measure would you use in the
customary system to measure the length of a celery stick?
Which units in the metric system?

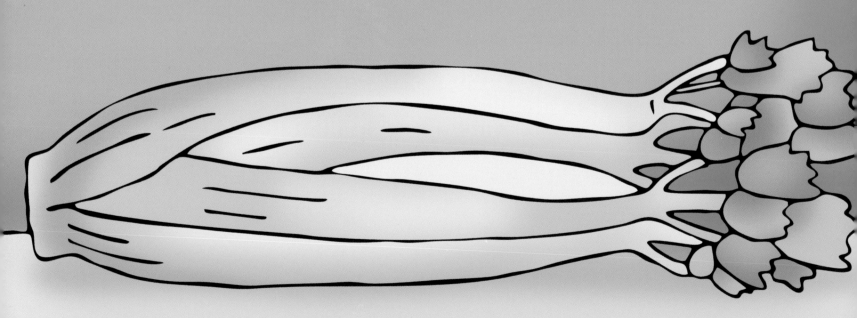

Which units would
you use to measure
the length of your kitchen?

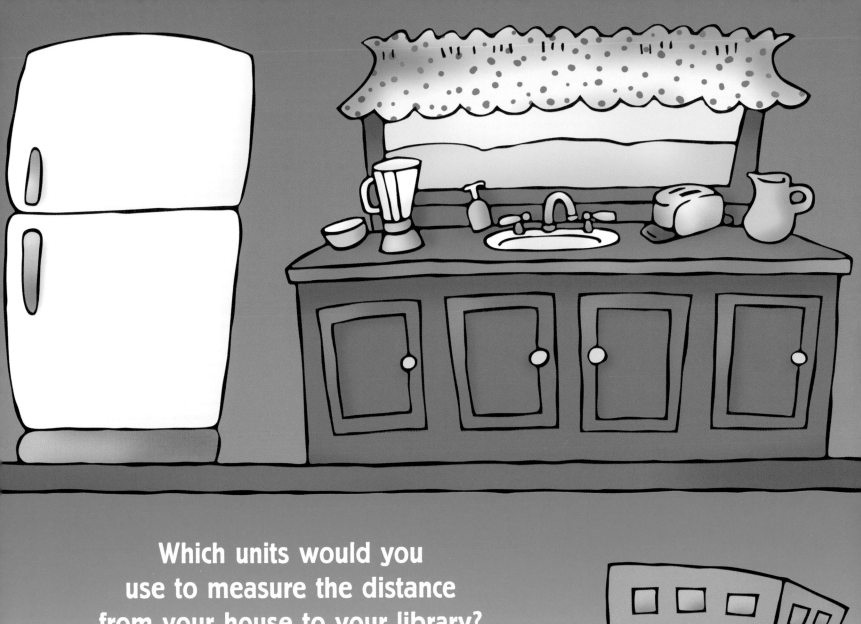

Which units would you use to measure the distance from your house to your library?

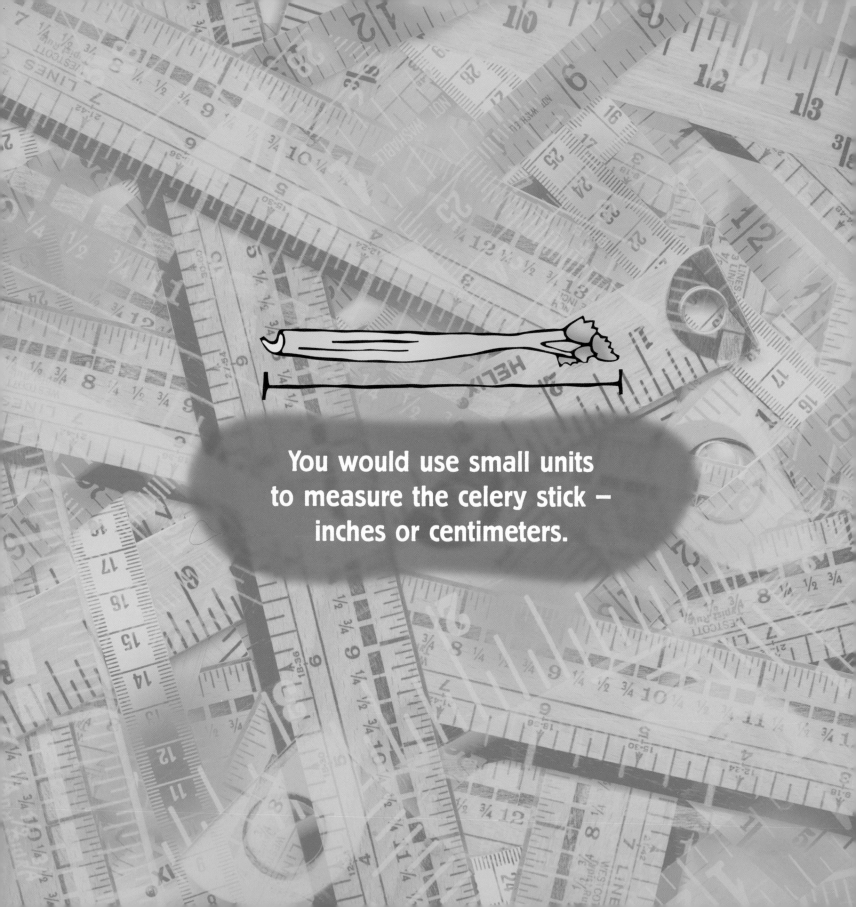

You would use small units
to measure the celery stick –
inches or centimeters.

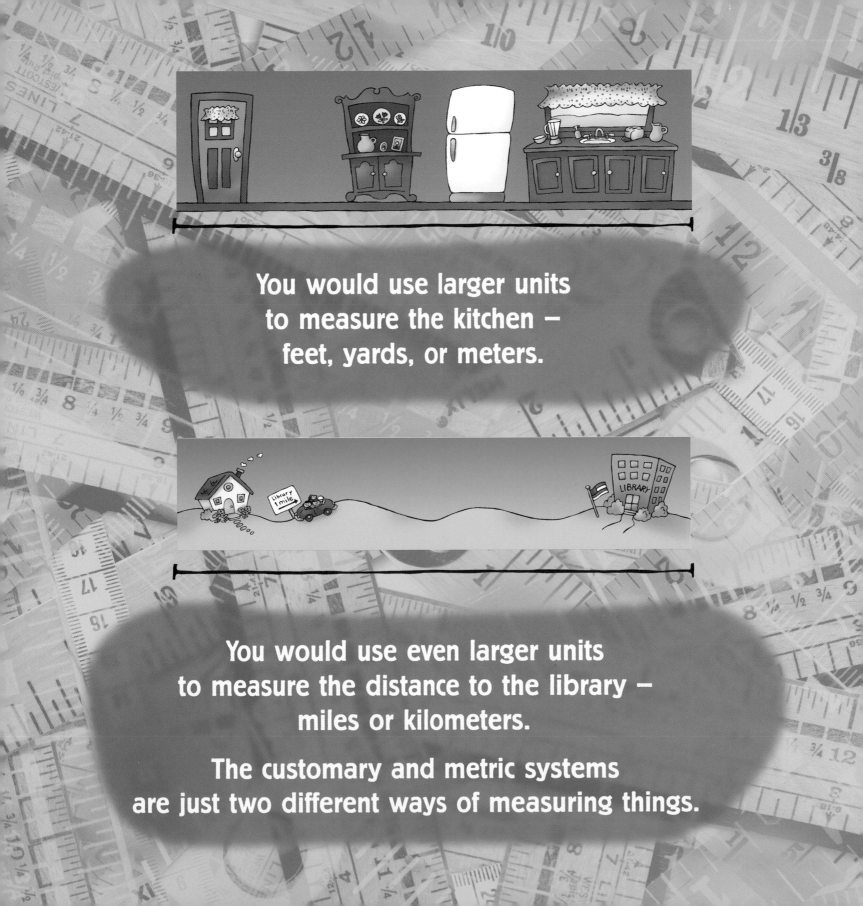

You would use larger units
to measure the kitchen —
feet, yards, or meters.

You would use even larger units
to measure the distance to the library —
miles or kilometers.

The customary and metric systems
are just two different ways of measuring things.

Get a pencil and a long
rectangular-shaped piece of cardboard
with two perfectly straight edges.

Place the cardboard's straight edge
alongside this 8-inch ruler and hold it there.
Copy the ruler's markings onto
the cardboard's straight edge.
You have made your own customary system ruler.

Now place the cardboard's
other straight edge alongside
this 20-centimeter ruler and hold it there.
Copy the markings and make your own metric ruler.

Use your ruler to measure
your pencil in inches and in centimeters.

Use it to measure a crayon, your bed,
and your pet's tail.

customary (inch)

metric

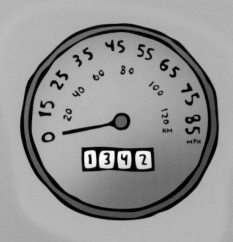

Go into a car and look at the speedometer. It probably measures speed in both miles-per-hour and kilometers-per-hour. The speedometer shows you that 25 miles-per-hour is about the same as 40 kilometers-per-hour. The odometer shows how far the car has traveled.

When you go for a ride, look at the signs you see on the highway. In many places distances are given in both miles and kilometers.

Check the odometer before you begin a ride. And when you're done, see how far you've traveled.

Inches and centimeters, feet, yards and meters, miles and kilometers, are just different ways of measuring the same length and distance.

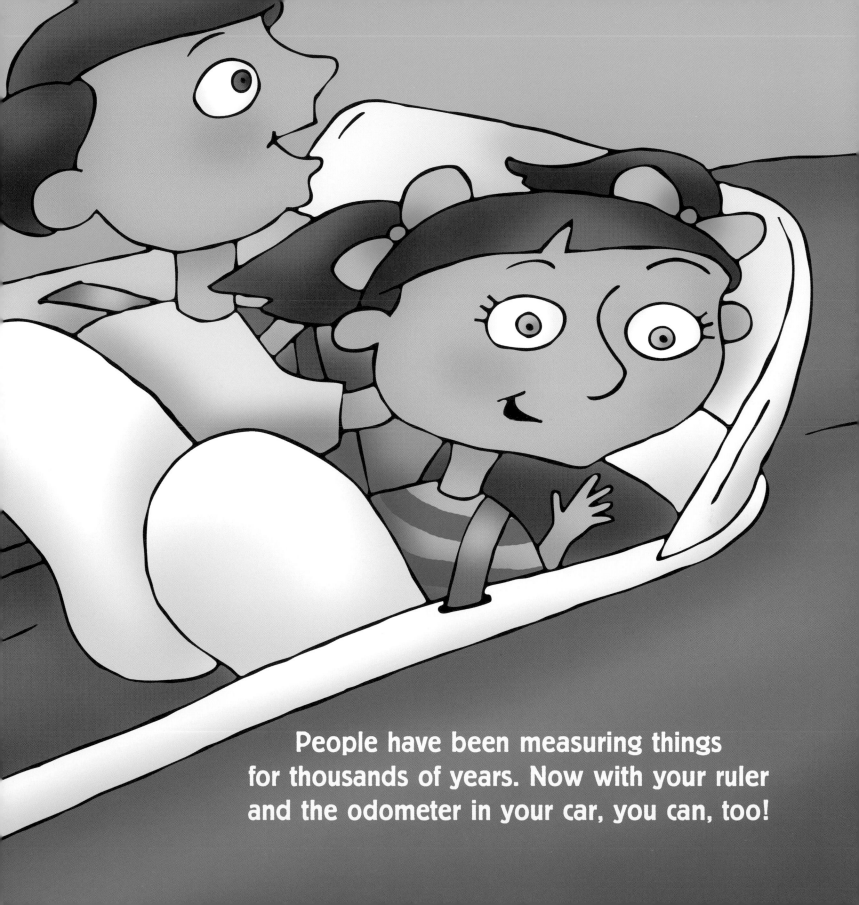

People have been measuring things
for thousands of years. Now with your ruler
and the odometer in your car, you can, too!

Conversion Tables

These tables will help you change
measurements from one system to the other.

1 inch ≅ 2.54 centimeters

1 foot ≅ 30.48 centimeters

1 yard (3 feet) ≅ 91.44 centimeters

1 mile ≅ 1.61 kilometers

1 centimeter ≅ 0.39 inches

1 meter ≅ 39.37 inches

1 kilometer ≅ 0.62 miles